Let's meet our First Grade teacher, Ms. Best!

Ms. Best

"Hello, my name is Ms. Best. I'm thrilled to welcome you to First Grade. You are unique, which means not like anyone else, and will learn at your own pace. Read this book with an adult, ask and answer questions, find Yodie the coyote and have fun! Let's meet six Cedar Valley Kids™!"

Barack

Chan

Minda

Sam

Dallas

Gabriella

Let's learn about vowels!

The letters in green are vowels. Let's point to and say each vowel, starting with A.

UPPERCASE LETTERS

A B C D E F G H
I J K L M N O P Q
R S T U V W X Y Z

lowercase letters

a b c d e f g h i
j k l m n o p q r
s t u v w x y z

"Can you say the vowels in your name? Good job!"

Let's learn about consonants!

The letters in blue are consonants. Let's point to and say each consonant, starting with B.

UPPERCASE LETTERS

A B C D E F G H I J K L M
N O P Q R S T U V W X Y Z

lowercase letters

a b c d e f g h
i j k l m n o p q
r s t u v w x y z

"Y can be a vowel or a consonant. The letter Y can make the ee sound as in happy, the i sound as in why and the yuh sound as in yes. Happy, why yes!"

Let's say the short ă sound!

Say apple, **a-a** apple. The **a-a** is the short ă sound.
Let's point to and s-t-r-e-t-c-h out (sound out) more
words with the short ă sound.

rămt   săd

hăt   plăn

glăd   rănch

străp   hătch

chămp   yăm

"What sound does the short ă make?
Thăt's right!"

Let's say the short ĕ sound!

Say egg, **e-e** egg. The **e-e** is the short ĕ sound. Let's point to and s-t-r-e-t-c-h out more words with the short ĕ sound.

rĕd   lĕg

tĕn   pĕt

lĕss   bĕst

shĕd   tĕst

blĕss   slĕd

shĕll   swĕpt

smĕll

"What sound does the short ĕ make? Yĕs!"

Let's say the short ĭ sound!

Say igloo, i-i igloo. The i-i is the short ĭ sound. Let's point to and s-t-r-e-t-c-h out more words with the short ĭ sound.

hĭp   fĭg   kĭd   hĭll

twĭg   skĭt   trĭp   spĭll

pĭtch

splĭt

drĭft

whĭsk

ship

"What sound does the short ĭ make? Hĭp hĭp hurray!"

Let's say the short ŏ sound!

Say octopus, **o-o** octopus. The **o-o** is the short ŏ sound.
Let's point to and s-t-r-e-t-c-h out more words with the short ŏ sound.

mŏm	tŏt	pŏd	lŏp	hŏt
jŏb	nŏt	shŏp		
plŏt	blŏb			
clŏck	trŏt			

"What sound does
the short ŏ make?
You've got it!"

Let's say the short ŭ sound!

Say umbrella, **u-u** umbrella. The **u-u** sound is the short ŭ sound. Let's point to and s-t-r-e-t-c-h out more words with the short ŭ sound.

hŭg	bŭs	gŭm
pŭp	mŭg	slŭg
rŭb	plŭm	clŭck
lŭnch	chŭm	
scrŭb	plŭck	

"What sound does the short ŭ make? That's fŭn!"

Let's say the long ā, ī, ō and ū sounds!

By adding **e** at the end of the blue words, the a, i, o and u say their names, the long vowel sound. Let's say the short vowel sounds in the blue words and then change to the long vowel sounds in the words with the red e at the end.

short	long	short	long
căn	cāne	nŏt	nōte
răt	rāte	hŏp	hōpe
Săm	sāme	rŏd	rōde
dĭm	dīme	cŭt	cūte
kĭt	kīte	cŭb	cūbe

"We call the e at the end of these words silent e. Nice!"

Let's learn about word families!

A word family is a rhyming letter pattern. Point to and say the word families below.

ăt	ĕll	ĭll	ŏp	ŭnk	y
bat	bell	bill	hop	junk	by
hat	yell	pill	pop	bunk	cry
cat	tell	grill	flop	chunk	fly
mat	spell	spill		trunk	shy
flat					try

"Can you think of any more words that belong in these families? Swell!"

Let's learn about prefixes & suffixes!

A **prefix** is added to the beginning of a root word.	prefix		root word		
	re	+	read	=	reread
	un	+	zip	=	unzip

A **suffix** is added to the end of a root word.	root word		suffix		
	sing	+	er	=	singer
	howl	+	ing	=	howling

"A **prefix** or **suffix** + a root word = a new word. Unbelievably outstanding!"

Let's learn about contractions!

A contraction is the combination of two words. One or more letters are replaced by an apostrophe ('). Let's point to and say the words and the contractions in red.

I am   I'm

did not   didn't

you will   you'll

is not   isn't

they will   they'll

I will   I'll

it is   it's

where is   where's

she will   she'll

what is   what's

Let's learn about compound words!

A compound word is a **long** word made up of two or more shorter words.

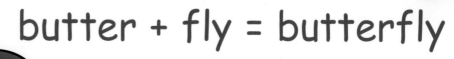

butter + fly = butterfly

cow + girl = cowgirl

bare + foot = barefoot

rattle + snake = rattlesnake

"What do we call a long word made up of two or more words? How **extraordinary**!"

Let's learn about capitalization!

We capitalize:

the first letter of a sentence **R**eading is fun!

special places **A**ustin, **T**exas

names of people **M**s. **B**est

the proper noun **I**

Yodie and I love to read.

"We also capitalize special events, holidays, titles, days of the week, the months of the year and more. Can you point to the capital letters on this page? Superb!"

Let's learn about punctuation!

We can end a sentence with a

period ●, question mark ? or exclamation mark !.

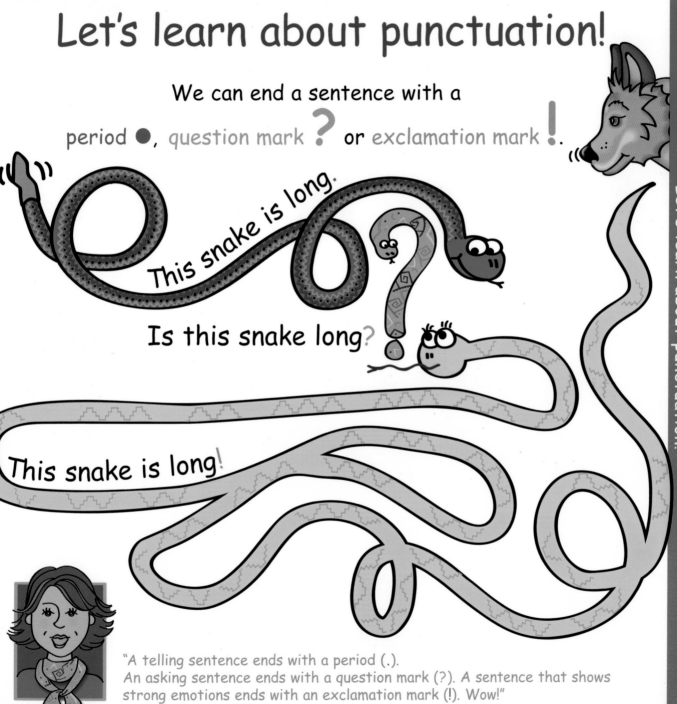

This snake is long.

Is this snake long?

This snake is long!

"A telling sentence ends with a period (.).
An asking sentence ends with a question mark (?). A sentence that shows strong emotions ends with an exclamation mark (!). Wow!"

Let's make some words plural!

Sometimes we make words "plural" by adding an **S**.
Plural means more than one. Let's look at some examples.

spider

spiders

girl

girls

hat

hats

"Splendid!"

Let's measure!

Centimeters

| 0 | 1 | 2 | 3 | 4 | 5 | 6 | 7 | 8 | 9 | 10 | 11 | 12 | 13 | 14 | 15 |

| 0 | 1 | 2 | 3 | 4 | 5 | 6 |

Inches

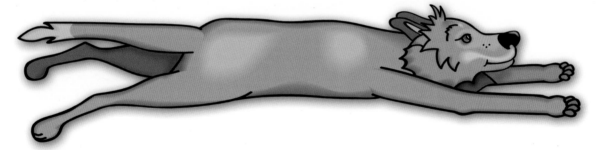

How many butterflies = 2 rattlesnakes?
How many rattlesnakes = 1 coyote?

Answers: 6 butterflies, 2 rattlesnakes.

"How many inches long is Yodie? How many centimeters long are 3 butterflies? Goodness snakes!"

Answers: 6 inches, 7 1/2 centimeters.

Let's name geometric shapes!

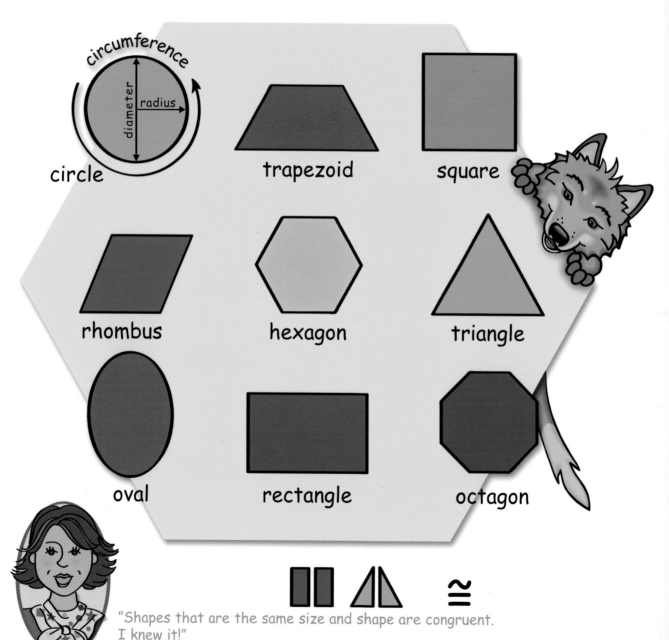

circumference

diameter

radius

circle

trapezoid

square

rhombus

hexagon

triangle

oval

rectangle

octagon

"Shapes that are the same size and shape are congruent.
I knew it!"

Let's name solid geometric shapes!

Let's point to and say each shape.
Are those shapes flat?
No, they are 3D!

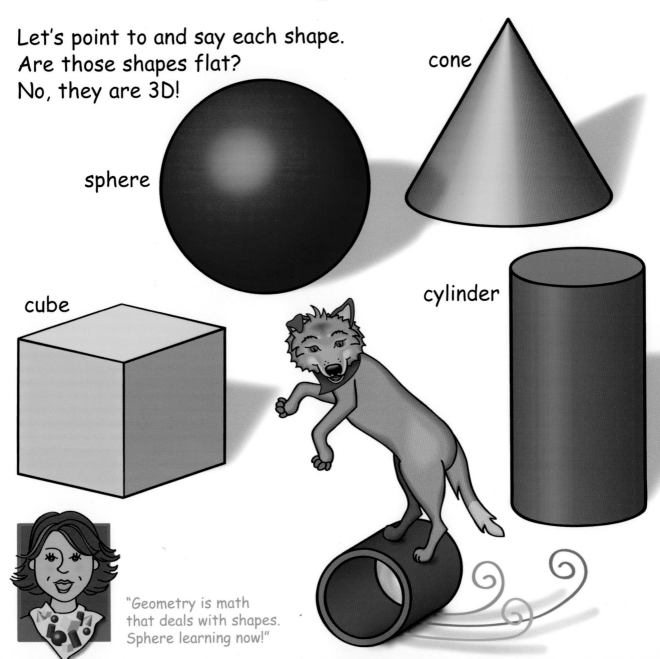

cone

sphere

cube

cylinder

"Geometry is math that deals with shapes. Sphere learning now!"

Let's count!

Let's point to and say each number word. Then let's count each item next to the number word.

zero

one

two

three

four

five

six

seven

eight

nine

ten

"Point to the number words 3, 7 and 9. That's fine!"

Let's learn about even and odd!

0 1 2 3 4 5 6 7 8 9

10 11 12 13 14 15 16 17 18 19

20 21 22 23 24 25 26 27 28 29

30 31 32 33 34 35 36 37 38 39

40 41 42 43 44 45 46 47 48 49

50 51 52 53 54 55 56 57 58 59

60 61 62 63 64 65 66 67 68 69

70 71 72 73 74 75 76 77 78 79

80 81 82 83 84 85 86 87 88 89

90 91 92 93 94 95 96 97 98 99

100

What pattern do you see?

"The red numbers are even numbers. The blue numbers are odd numbers. Let's point to and say the even numbers and then the odd. Fantastic!"

Let's skip count!

By 10s

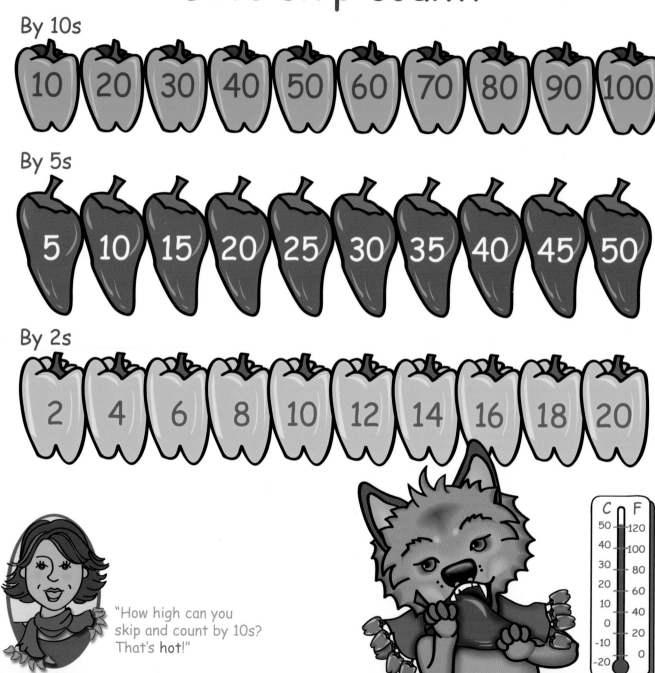

| 10 | 20 | 30 | 40 | 50 | 60 | 70 | 80 | 90 | 100 |

By 5s

| 5 | 10 | 15 | 20 | 25 | 30 | 35 | 40 | 45 | 50 |

By 2s

| 2 | 4 | 6 | 8 | 10 | 12 | 14 | 16 | 18 | 20 |

"How high can you skip and count by 10s? That's **hot**!"

Let's learn about ordinals!

The boots are in order. Let's say the ordinal numbers beginning with First.

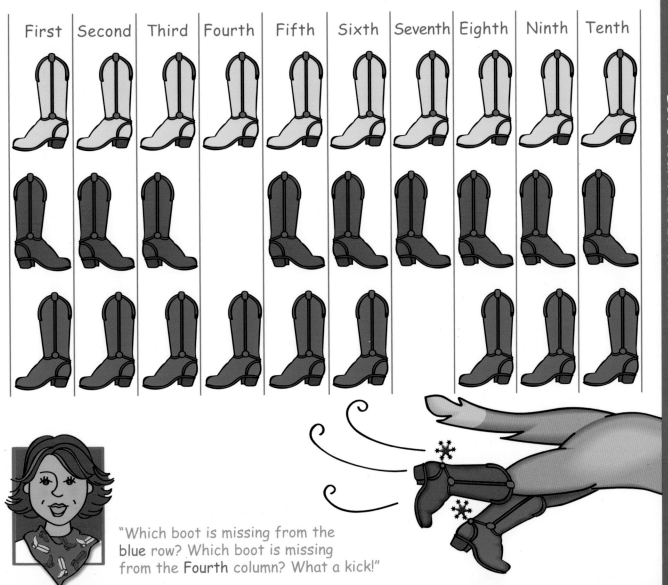

First	Second	Third	Fourth	Fifth	Sixth	Seventh	Eighth	Ninth	Tenth

"Which boot is missing from the blue row? Which boot is missing from the Fourth column? What a kick!"

Let's add!

Say the answer to each problem.

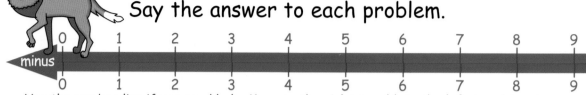

minus

0 1 2 3 4 5 6 7 8 9

0 1 2 3 4 5 6 7 8 9

Use the number line if you need help. Move to the right to add, to the left to subtract.

2 +2	1 +2	2 +1	3 +3	2 +4	4 +2
4 +4	4 +1	1 +4	5 +5	3 +4	4 +3
6 +6	2 +5	5 +2	7 +7	5 +4	4 +5
8 +8	6 +3	3 +6	9 +9	3 +7	7 +3

"That really adds up!"

addend   addend   sum   is the
10 + 10 = 20   same as

10 addend
+10 addend
20 sum

Let's subtract!
Say the answer to each problem.

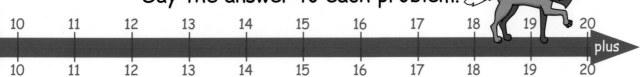

10 11 12 13 14 15 16 17 18 19 20 plus
10 11 12 13 14 15 16 17 18 19 20

2 -1	5 -3	5 -2	3 -2	6 -2	6 -4
4 -3	7 -2	7 -5	5 -1	8 -3	8 -5
6 -3	9 -4	9 -5	7 -3	10 -6	10 -4
8 -2	10 -5	12 -6	9 -3	14 -7	16 -8

"Minuend, subtrahend, (clap, clap) difference!"

minuend subtrahend difference
10   -   3   =   7

is the same as

10 minuend
-3 subtrahend
7   difference

Let's learn about fractions!

When a "whole" is divided into equal (the same size) parts, the parts are called fractions. Let's count the number of equal parts shaded and then the total number of equal parts, and say each fraction.

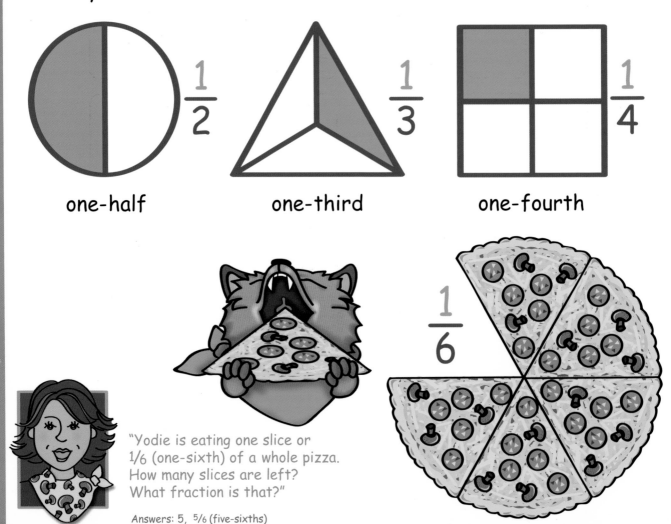

$\frac{1}{2}$ one-half

$\frac{1}{3}$ one-third

$\frac{1}{4}$ one-fourth

$\frac{1}{6}$

"Yodie is eating one slice or 1/6 (one-sixth) of a whole pizza. How many slices are left? What fraction is that?"

Answers: 5, 5/6 (five-sixths)

Let's use a graph!

Yodie took a walk. He counted scorpions, lizards and butterflies. Yodie then made a graph to show what he saw and how many.

How Many Yodie Saw

10
9
8
7
6
5
4
3
2

scorpions   lizards   butterflies

What Yodie Saw

"How many scorpions, lizards and butterflies did Yodie count? Leaping lizards!"

Answers: 10 scorpions, 4 lizards and 7 butterflies

Let's learn about food groups!

Let's point to and say each food group.

Let's learn about food groups!

For more information,
please visit www.mypyramid.gov

"Your body is like an engine. It needs good fuel (food)
to work well. What healthy foods do you eat?" Yummy!

Let's learn about our internal organs!

Internal organs are inside our bodies. Let's point to and say each internal organ starting with the brain.

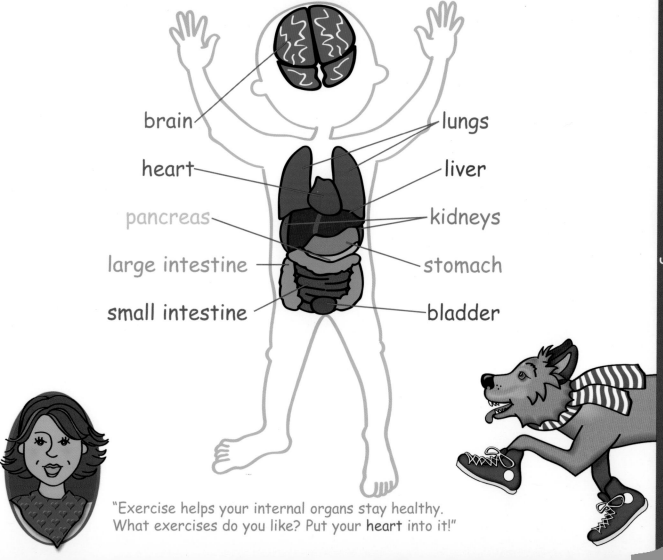

brain

heart

pancreas

large intestine

small intestine

lungs

liver

kidneys

stomach

bladder

"Exercise helps your internal organs stay healthy. What exercises do you like? Put your **heart** into it!"

Let's look at money!

$0.01 = 1¢ penny

$0.05 = 5¢ nickel

$0.10 = 10¢ dime

$0.25 = 25¢ quarter

$1.00 dollar

"Let's name the presidents on the coins, starting with the penny. By George, I think you've got it!"

Answers: Abraham Lincoln (sixteenth president), Thomas Jefferson (third president), Franklin Roosevelt (thirty-fourth president) & George Washington (first president).

Let's add money!

Let's point to and add each row of coins.

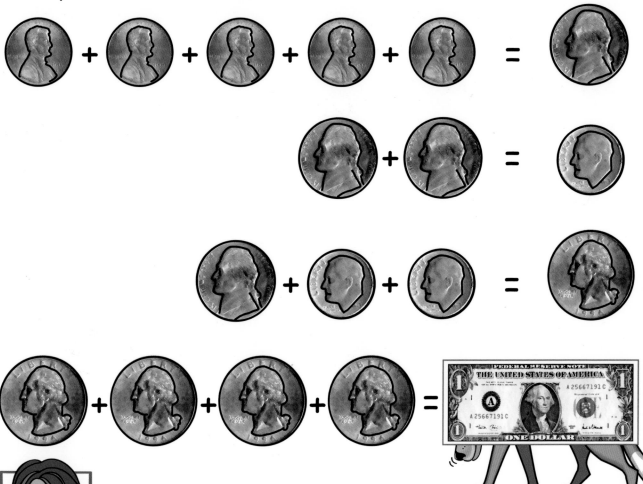

"Which coin is worth the most? Which coin is worth the least?
You are right on the money!"

Answers: quarter, penny

Let's read about day and night!

Our planet Earth constantly spins. As we spin or revolve in the Sun's light, it is day. As we revolve out of the Sun's light, it is night.

Sun

Earth

Day   Night

The Earth makes a complete rotation every 24 hours. That's one day!

"Slowly spin a globe in front of a light, and you'll see why we have day and night. You're so bright!"

Let's learn about our solar system!

Nine planets and the Sun make up our solar system. These nine planets form an ellipse or oval pattern around the massive yellow Sun. Let's point to and say each planet.

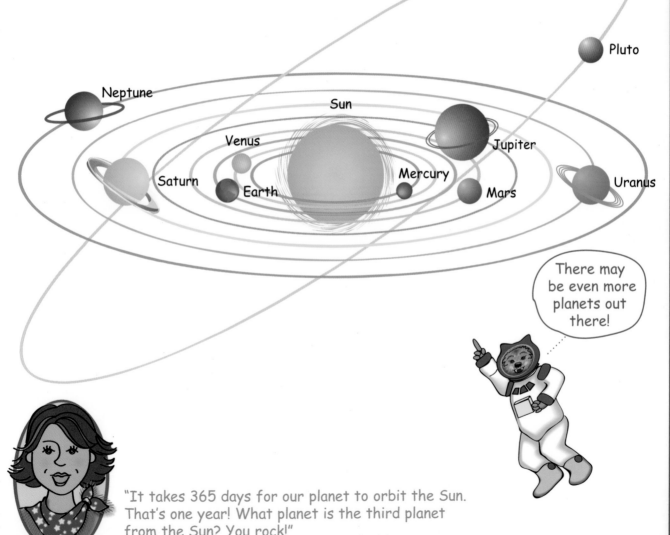

There may be even more planets out there!

"It takes 365 days for our planet to orbit the Sun. That's one year! What planet is the third planet from the Sun? You rock!"

Let's learn some words!

Let's learn some words!

what   will   jump   they   with

up   out   some   him   little   can   their

of   his   had   but   as   down

were   am   there   friend

do   all   BIG   she   then

her   yes   so   when

"Most of these words we learn to recognize by sight, not by sounding them out. Out of sight!"

Let's read a story!

The Fang Fairy, Author: Fuzz E. One

"Hurray! I lost my first fang," said Yodie, excitedly. "I will put it under my pillow, and the hairy, but beautiful, Fang Fairy will take my fang and leave a bone."

Yodie quickly took a bath, brushed and flossed his fangs and jumped into bed. He fell fast asleep. That magical night the Fang Fairy appeared.

Moments later she departed, leaving a trail of shimmering sparkles and a few tiny fleas. Yodie woke up the next morning. He checked under his pillow and said, "The Fang Fairy left TWO shiny bones!" Crunch! Crunch!

"Why was Yodie excited?
What trail did the Fang Fairy leave?
Who was the author?
Have you lost any fangs?
Have you lost any teeth? Magnificent!"

The End

Let's tell time!

The short hand tells the hour, and the long hand tells the minute. Each shaded area is a quarter of an hour or 15 minutes. Let's point to the four small clocks and tell the time.

9:00

1:15

4:30

6:45

"Let's skip count by fives (clockwise) around the clock. We just counted the minutes in an hour! Time flies when you're having fun!"

Let's make a calendar!

Let's say the months of the year. Let's say the days of the week.

| January |
| February |
| March |
| April |
| May |
| June |
| July |
| August |
| September |
| October |
| November |
| December |

Month:				Year:		
Sunday	Monday	Tuesday	Wednesday	Thursday	Friday	Saturday

What's your weather like today?

"What is the weather like each month? Cool!"

Let's learn about colors!

Let's point to and say the primary and secondary colors below.

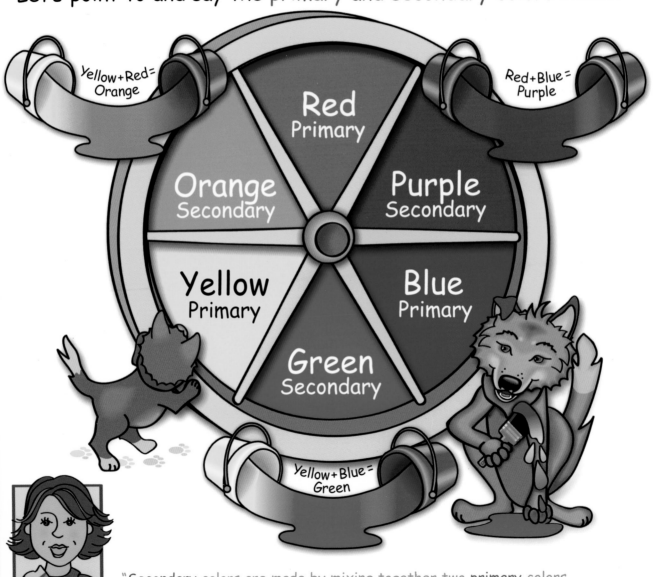

Yellow+Red=
Orange

Red+Blue=
Purple

Red
Primary

Orange
Secondary

Purple
Secondary

Yellow
Primary

Blue
Primary

Green
Secondary

Yellow+Blue=
Green

"Secondary colors are made by mixing together two primary colors.
What's your favorite color? Spectacular!"

Let's learn about our government!

Let's point to and say the three branches of our government.

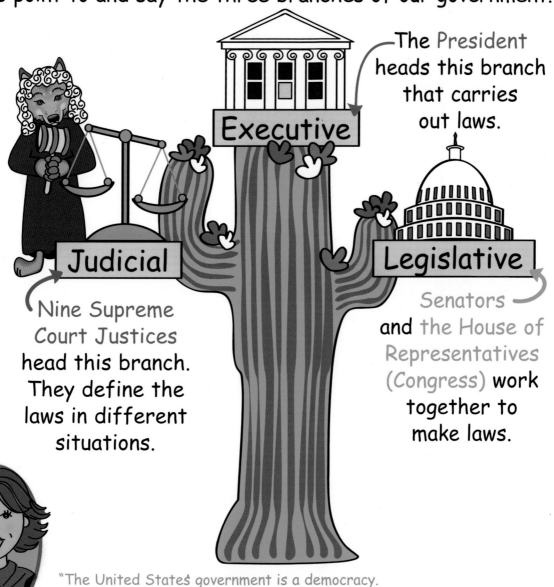

Executive

The President heads this branch that carries out laws.

Judicial

Nine Supreme Court Justices head this branch. They define the laws in different situations.

Legislative

Senators and the House of Representatives (Congress) work together to make laws.

"The United States government is a democracy. The people choose officials by voting. Yea!"

Let's practice writing!

Let's look at the stages of reading!

1	Recognize and name the alphabet in/out of sequence	abcdefg dacfbfe
2	Recognize letter sounds	b makes the "buh, buh" sound
3	Read phonetically, sounding out words and using decoding skills	c-a-t
4	Use picture clues, beginning sounds, ending sounds and letter combinations to decipher new words	"cuh, cuh cac tus cactus"